Quick Fix Your Life

The small changes that make a big difference

Quick Fix Your Life

Judith Verity

How To Books

Published by How To Books Ltd,
3 Newtec Place, Magdalen Road,
Oxford OX4 1RE. United Kingdom.
Tel: (01865) 793806. Fax: (01865) 248780.
email: info@howtobooks.co.uk
http://www.howtobooks.co.uk

British Library Cataloguing in Publication Data.

A catalogue record for this book is available from the British
Library.   370·1 VER

Cover design by Shireen Nathoo Design, London
Cover illustration by Roger Langridge
Cartoons by Grizelda Grizlingham

Produced for How To Books by Deer Park Productions
Design and Typeset by Shireen Nathoo Design, London
Printed and bound in Great Britain

NOTE: The material contained in this book is set out in good faith
for general guidance and no liability can be accepted for loss or
expense incurred as a result of relying in particular circumstances
on statements made in the book. Laws and regulations are
complex and liable to change, and readers should check the
current position with the relevant authorities before making
personal arrangements.

Contents

About the Author

Judith Verity has been in the Life
Changing and Personal Development
business for thirty years. She now writes
for the Human Capital Resources group of
trainers, counsellors and musicians.

Preface

This book is an introduction to some of the most useful ideas and exercises I've picked up during my 30 years in the self help business. Looking at the size of it, you might think it doesn't amount to much – but size isn't everything. The whole idea of Quick Fix is that you can do it and then spend the rest of the 23 hours and 50 minutes a day doing something interesting, exciting or profitable.

Maybe you feel your life could be better – but there's no way you could read enough self-help books to solve all the problems. If you don't have enough time to sleep, eat, empty the bins and talk to your friends – you aren't likely to squeeze in a couple of hours self improvement as well. But you might just spare ten minutes out of every 1,440 to introduce a few positive changes.

But if there are ten chapters in this book and ten minutes' worth of ideas in every chapter doesn't that add up to an hour and forty minutes a day? Well, yes it does, but you don't have to do them all every day!

The Quick Fix won't turn you into a higher spiritual being or set you on the path to world domination. But it will tell you very precisely how to make the small changes that mean a lot. And small changes add up. After all, we're talking about every area of your life, from keeping fit, sleeping soundly and organising your

diary, to rearranging your bedroom.

And there's a spin-off. Not only will you feel better, have more time and enjoy warmer relationships with your partner and your pets (massage section), you can also feel smug about running your life according to the fashions of the moment – Tai Chi, Feng Shui, Time Management – it's all here.

The great thing, however, is that it isn't all there is. Every chapter is just a peep into a world of possibilities. Of course, before you start doing any exercises, mental or physical, that you haven't tried before you should always check with your doctor first. It is your responsibility to make sure that you stay within your own safety and comfort zones.

None of the ideas or suppositions in this book have any meaning other than the meaning you give them.

None of these exercises have any value other than their value to you – and you won't know what that is until you check them out.

A lot of books promise to change your life. Only you can do that.

Judith Verity

Chapter One

Take a Deep Breath

*If all else fails remember this – keep breathing until
the situation improves.*
MARTY McGONAGAL

BENEFITS

* Deep breathing is good for your health.

* It has a calming effect and releases
  endorphins.

* Concentration on your breathing drives
  other thoughts from your mind and
  gives you a break from your worries.

BONUS

* Do it in downtime, in buses, trains,
  queues and boring meetings.

Considering that breathing is essential, it's amazing how we take it for granted. Unless we happen to be asthmatic, or allergic, or we catch a cold.

Not only do we take it for granted, most of us don't do it properly. Often our breathing is so shallow that we get out of breath walking upstairs or unloading a shopping trolley. It's not just because we don't get enough exercise – even when we work out we are often panting to get enough air into our lungs. Panting is for dogs. If you're exercising at the right level, you should be able to do it and breathe adequately through your mouth at the same time.

Taking a Breather

I was working in a big city office recently, it was a beautiful Spring day and I took my coffee out onto the fire escape to get away from the air conditioning. My heart sank when I saw the door open and the smokers trooping out. They all lit up and took their first long drag. I suddenly realised that they looked exactly like a meditation class centring themselves for a mind-clearing exercise.

'You don't breathe like that when you aren't smoking', I said.

'There's not much point unless you're inhaling something that gives you a buzz', said the Head of Accounts.

'Try it', I suggested, 'without the cigarette this time.'

They decided to humour me. Without the nicotine, they still had the same look of contentment as they took their deep breaths. We took a vote and they all agreed – deep breathing without the tobacco was not as good, but it was pretty good. Plus it was a lot cheaper.

Breathing Lying Down

2 Minutes

~ Lie down, on the bed or the floor.

~ Put both hands on your lower ribcage with fingers pointing inwards, not quite touching.

~ Inhale – your fingers will move up and apart.

~ Breathe deeply through your nose and feel your chest expand, your stomach rise and your ribs push outwards. Be aware of how far down that breath goes into your body. Hold that deep breath for as long as it's comfortable.

~ Let the breath go, let out all the air you took in. Your stomach subsides, your ribs sink back, the air drifts out.

~ Do two of these deep breaths and then relax and take a couple of normal ones. Two more deep ones and you're ready to get up and go.

Sit-Up breathing

2 Minutes

This exercise is done in a sitting position. It takes a little more concentration, but you can do it almost anywhere. After all, it's probably not a good idea to lie down in the middle of the office to do your breathing exercises.

~ Sit up, deportment style, with your spine straight (not rigid).

~ Relax your shoulders – they shouldn't move up and down.

~ Keep your hands loosely on your lap – you can place them on your lower ribcage just for the first breath, to check

that you're inhaling as deeply as when
you were lying down.

~ Take the two deep breaths in and out,
relax for a couple of normal breaths
and repeat the deep ones.

~ Let your ribs move, keep your shoulders
still.

Walking and Breathing

4 Minutes

~ Don't laugh. Not everybody can do this.

~ Walk at a steady pace, wait until you have got into your stride.

~ Breathe in, deeply, for two paces.

~ Hold that breath for two paces.

~ Breathe out for two paces.

~ Repeat the breathing five times (you may find you continue for longer, almost automatically).

23

Sun and Moon Breathing

3 Minutes

A lot of breathing exercises come from
yoga – in which breath control is very
important. So some of them have exotic
names. The sun and moon represent *yang*
and *yin*, symbols of positive and negative,
or light and dark. It sounds so romantic
that I couldn't resist giving its Eastern
name. But if you want to stay firmly down
to earth you could call this routine *One-
Nostril Breathing* or *Left and Right
Breathing*.

Why call it anything at all? All the
exercises in this book have names, it's like
labelling the jars in the cupboard – so you
can find the right one in a hurry.

24

~ Sit on the floor with your legs crossed if you can do it easily. If you haven't sat cross-legged on the floor since you were in the scouts, don't attempt it now without qualified help at hand. You can also do this exercise sitting normally on a chair with both feet on the floor.

~ Hold one nostril shut and breathe through the other. Use the muscles in your nose to open that nostril wider as you breathe.

~ Change sides and breathe through the other nostril.

~ When you've got the hang of it start counting.

~ To a count of three, breathe in through
   your right nostril.

~ Hold it for a count of three.

~ Breathe out to a count of three.

~ Do the same on the left side.

~ Do this twice both sides.

Breathing Away Stress

4 Minutes

~ Stand rigidly upright with your hands by your side and fists clenched.

~ Tense all your muscles and slowly breathe in as you rise up onto your toes.

~ Hold the breath for a count of three, shoulders hunched, muscles contracted. Find a point ahead of you to stare at and this will help you keep your balance.

~ As you start to breathe out, slowly relax all your muscles from your neck to your toes, lowering your feet flat on the

27

floor. You should be in the Orang Utan
position with droopy hands, sloping
shoulders and bent knees.

~ Do this five times.

HOW TO...

* Link this with something you do regularly so that the thing you do triggers your breathing exercise. This is called anchoring. You might use your tea break, your bed-time routine, waiting at the station twice a day or queuing at the supermarket.

* Print out the routines on pieces of paper and stick them up where you want to use them. The bathroom mirror, the inside of your briefcase, the dashboard of the car...

...DO IT

* Pick one or two of these exercises that come easily to you and do them at least once a day.

* Don't do more than 10 minutes *conscious* breathing a day – like all the exercises in this book, it's a means to an end, not an end in itself. Get a life.

Chapter Two

Tai Chi in the Morning

I don't do mornings
GARFIELD

BENEFITS

* Tai Chi gets you moving easily in the morning.

* It tones you up and calms you down without wearing you out.

BONUS

* You don't need special clothes, but bare feet are better than high heels. Work boots, Gucci loafers or trainers are fine too.

* You needn't be sweating and exhausted with Tai Chi so you could do a few of the forms in the park on the way to work.

* In some parts of the world (New York and Shanghai for example) you can do a bit of Tai Chi right outside your office wearing your street clothes. It's still considered eccentric in Europe, but on the other hand it's always been fashionable to be eccentric.

Be still as a mountain, move like a great river
WU YU-HSIANG

Isn't that inspiring? Like the Sun and Moon breathing in the last chapter, it brings a simple idea to life. *Chi* is energy and Tai Chi is about combining the energy of the earth with the energy of the heavens (back to Yin and Yang, the strength and balance of Darkness and Light again).

Tai Chi uses stillness to control movement, which makes for a beautifully balanced state of body and mind. Life in the modern world is an unhealthy combination of physical inactivity and mental turmoil.

Zen and the Art of Motorcycle Maintenance

When I first started to ride a motorbike I was worried about controlling my tiny Yamaha when I was whizzing along at 40 miles an hour. (I was pretty sure I wouldn't be doing 70 straight away.) I needn't have worried. I spent ages making tiny, wobbly, figures of eight in a disused carpark – hardly the glamorous image I'd hoped for. After half a day of frustration and boredom, when I had the distinct feeling that I was getting worse, not better, I protested to the instructor.

'Couldn't we go out on the road now – after all, I'm not going to be going round

in circles at 10 miles an hour on the M4,
am I?'

I obviously wasn't the first to complain.
He looked at me and said, 'Combining the
slowest movement with the greatest
control is the hardest lesson to learn. If
you can do that, you can do anything.'

A couple of hours later we went out in
the traffic. And when I had to make an
uphill, standing start at traffic lights with a
bus on either side, and a queue of
impatient car drivers behind, I realised
what he meant.

More Hara, Less Kiri

2 Minutes

~ Stand up and put your thumb on your navel, your *Hara* is three fingers' width below that. It's also called the *Tan t'ien*. Besides being the correct place to ritually disembowel yourself, the Hara is also the point of balance for martial arts and meditation routines.

~ Think about something that annoys you. No big deal, just a minor irritation. Make pictures of it in your head. How do you feel when you do that? Would it be a good state to be in if you were under threat?

~ Next, focus your attention down in your Hara. Feel the balancing point of your body there, where your weight is concentrated in the pit of your stomach. When you are centred on your Hara, picture your petty irritation again and feel the difference. Does it still upset you as much? Probably not.

This is a powerful way to focus your mind on your body. It strengthens you mentally and physically. Here's another way to test it out with the help of a friend.

~ Tell your friend to picture in his head someone or something that upsets him. When he has something in mind, gently push his shoulder – you'll find he is easily swayed.

~ Next ask him to focus on his Hara before he makes the annoying picture and push him again. What difference do you notice? What difference does he feel?

~ This is why the Hara or Tan t'ien is so important in martial arts. It's where you must be based if you want to be strong.

Carpe Diem

2 Minutes

Seize your day. Don't wait for it to sneak up and grab you. Crawling out of bed to the kettle is not assertive. Starting with Tai Chi is one option of many, but if you really are with Garfield on mornings maybe you should consider one of the other chapters and quit on this one. On the other hand, these exercises might change the way you start the day – and you know what they say about getting off to a good start.

~ As soon as you wake up, or sooner – *conscious* participation isn't necessary, just as long as your body's moving –

put on the track suit you put out the
night before and go outside. Imagine a
beautiful dawn, you are standing in
bare feet on cool wet grass, near
running water and tall trees. Wouldn't
that be perfect? But a balcony with a
few pot plants is fine – or even your
bedroom floor if it's snowing or you're
housebound.

~ Stand up and take a deep breath, right
down into your diaphragm. Locate your
Hara and breathe into that. Centre
yourself on your Hara.

~ Think about your feet and how heavy
they are. In the middle of the ball of
each foot are your *Yung Ch'uan* points –

41

imagine that these points on the soles of your feet are rooted to the ground. This gives you a very strong, safe connection to the earth.

~ Now that you have the connection, and the stillness, you can start to move.

Greeting the Sun

6 Minutes

~ Stand with your feet shoulders width apart and your weight evenly spread between them. This is the base position.

~ Raise your right arm above your head with the elbow bent and shift your weight onto your right leg. Then lower your arm and change sides. Raise your left arm with the elbow bent and shift your weight onto the left leg. Next, clasp your hands and push them out in front of you at shoulder level. Return to your base position.

~ Put your hands on your hips and take a deep breath. Shift your weight on to your right leg and turn your waist, arms and upper body to the left, bending the left knee slightly and keeping your back straight. Then transfer your weight to the left leg and turn your upper body to the right, bending your right knee slightly. Return to your base position.

~ Balance your weight evenly between both legs again and clasp your hands. Raise both your arms and put your hands, still clasped, behind your head Bend forward, slowly from the waist until your head is level with your knees. With your head still at knee level, shift your weight to your left leg

and turn your waist to the left. Raise
your upper body to a standing position
while you are still facing left. Return to
base position and repeat the whole
exercise turning to the right.

~ Return to base position, stand and
   breathe deeply.

Between every movement, pause and
breathe until you are ready to move again.

HOW TO...

* Balance every Tai Chi movement or form by sinking your energy into your Hara. This gives you grace and balance.

* Every movement should be combined with stillness. The slower the better.

...DO IT

* Take these movements slowly and breathe deeply through them. These are not aerobic exercise routines.

Chapter Three

Other People

Hell is other people.
JEAN PAUL SARTRE

Hell, madam, is to love no more.
GEORGES BERNANOS

BENEFITS

* You can't change other people – but you can change the way you feel about them.

* When you change the way you feel about other people, you sometimes start to feel a whole lot better about yourself.

BONUS

* Do it in downtime, in buses, trains,
  queues and boring meetings.

Wouldn't it be great if you lived and worked with happy, cheerful, life-enhancing people who loved you to bits? Well, maybe you could, maybe you should, maybe you do.

The exercise I'm describing here was taught to me years ago in a meditation class and since then I've used it in my personal life as well as in business situations. Recently, I was talking to George, who came to see me about his staff problems. George works for a big company, and because he was technically so good at his job, he'd been made Head of Department before he was thirty. Unfortunately, although he was brilliant at the technical stuff, he wasn't the greatest people manager.

George's biggest difficulties were with his trainees; he just couldn't keep the first jobbers for more than a couple of months. When I asked him what was going wrong, he said: 'They never do what they're supposed to do, they're disorganised, unmotivated and they don't seem to have any commitment to their work'.

I used to work for the same company and I told him that I could remember a high conversion rate from trainees to permanent junior executive level – 'Even the temps used to sign up for permanent jobs when they came available,' I reminded him.

He shook his head. 'The HR Department must be sending me the rejects then.' The conversation was going nowhere, so I decided to take him through the *Tie Breaker* exercise.

The Tie Breaker

3 – 10 Minutes

Select one of the problem relationships in your life. Just a minor one for practice – don't go for big issues first time around. Maybe somebody at work is irritating you. Maybe it's a neighbour, or a relative. Don't try sorting out big feelings around children or parents or partners just yet – wait until you're really comfortable with doing it.

The Tie Breaker is a visualisation technique and you will need to go inside yourself. If that's a place you don't visit very often, now is a good time to start. People often tell me they don't make pictures – but everybody does. Don't you ever dream? And if I ask you the colour of your front door, you will almost certainly see it – if only for a second.

Picture yourself in a light bubble. Have you seen any sci fi movies recently? Power shields, time-warps and other universes always seem to be inside giant soap bubbles. The hero pushes one hand tentatively against it and it engulfs him (or her). All the Special Effects Departments seem to be coming up with the same idea at the moment – they must have spent a lot of time blowing bubbles when they were children.

~ So, if you can think of something more imaginative, go for it. Otherwise use the first giant, rainbow-coloured, soap bubble that floats by. What colour is the light in the bubble? Can you see yourself clearly, sitting safely, calmly inside it?

~ Now another bubble drifts along and in it, of course, is the person with whom you have an issue. Your personal Difficult Person. What colour is their bubble? What is the DP wearing? How do they look? Calm? Anxious? Aggressive?

~ If the DP stands up, ask them to sit down. It's important that you have their whole attention.

~ Let the bubbles float together, when you are ready. They will merge.

~ Now you are sitting in a rainbow bubble, opposite your DP. Notice that you are actually joined to them by a string, ribbon, rope, or chain. Sometimes it's so thin you can hardly see it at all. Sometimes it's heavy enough to tether a raging bull. Notice where you are joined. Is it ankle to ankle, or wrist to wrist or neck and neck?

~ Ask yourself, 'how do I feel?' Smile at your DP and ask them what they want from you.

~ Wait for an answer. If you don't get one, ask again.

~ You may not get a verbal answer – they might give you something, or do something. Whatever you get, thank them for it. Acknowledge their comment or gesture.

~ Now for the dramatic bit. Take whatever you need – scissors, a Stanley knife, a pair of shears, a ceremonial sword, or even some bolt cutters – and sever that connection. Whatever joins you to the other person, whether it's a cobweb or a chain, when *you* are ready, you can break it.

~ As soon as you've cut the connection, split the bubble again and sit for a moment totally separated. Then, let the DP float safely away in their bubble, surrounded by light.

George's Bubble

For George, running through the Tie Breaker with his latest trainee in one bubble and himself in the other was quite dramatic. When he asked the trainee what he wanted, the answer came to him straight away: 'a proper job description, some support and some feedback'.

He could see immediately that he wasn't giving his new staff the direction and guidance they needed, firstly because he was young and lacked confidence himself and, secondly, because he was too lazy to take the time to write up a job description and input the training time. Not surprisingly, the recruits felt confused and uncomfortable, and didn't do a good job.

Warning: it doesn't always work as well as this first time

But then again, sometimes it does. This exercise improves with practice. If you don't get clear insight and instant relief first time around, persevere. Do it again immediately or leave a few hours or a day in between. Sometimes it will re-run itself, unannounced, when you aren't expecting it – just before a meeting with the Difficult Person, or in a dream that stays in your mind when you wake up.

It's always worth a couple of minutes of your time. Even a fleeting negative encounter – losing your temper with the driver in front of you at the lights who doesn't immediately spot them turning green – can make you feel bad for ten minutes. Yet the original incident lasted only a few seconds. Practise the Tie Breaker on life's petty aggravations and then, when you're ready, you can tackle the big stuff.

HOW TO...

* Let what comes to you during this exercise come. Don't force it – you'll know whether you're getting a real answer or not.

* There's nothing spiritual or mystical about this (unless you're that way inclined). It's merely a device for getting in touch with your own unconscious so that you can access useful information.

* There are as many versions of this exercise as people who do it. I recently met up with my original meditation group and, when we got to talking about the Tie Breaker, I was amazed at

how many different ways it could be used. Feel free to improvise and develop your own.

...DO IT

* Practise when you are alone and can concentrate. Eventually it will become so fast and automatic that you'll be running it in the middle of meetings, or even before you make a call to your DP.

Chapter Four

Calmer Karma and Total Relaxation

You fill up my senses, like a night in the forest...
JOHN DENVER

BENEFITS

* Health, wealth, happiness and a perfect smile.

* The ability to relax deeply whenever you want reduces the risk of stress-related illness (just about everything is stress-related, from asthma to cancer, according to some current research).

* It makes exams easier to pass – people often fail through nervousness rather than lack of knowledge.

* It eliminates stress at work, so you get ahead while everybody else gets a headache.

* Relaxing in social situations attracts other happy, well-balanced people, so your personal life blossoms.

* Knowing you can relax in the dentist's chair makes you more likely to have regular checkups.

I can't *guarantee* all these good things for you when you use the Rainbow exercise (page 77), but regular relaxation will certainly make you feel better more of the time.

BONUS

* Do it in downtime, in buses, trains, queues, boring meetings.

* Results are instant – once you have mastered a relaxation technique that works for you, you can activate it in seconds.

I f you've ever had the misfortune (or benefit, depending on whether it worked), of receiving psychiatric treatment, you'll know there are four kinds of therapy: drugs, talking, ECT and relaxation.

Relaxation is the only non-controversial remedy for all forms of anxiety. Acceptable to most psychiatric disciplines, it's quick, cheap and has no adverse side effects. It's available free on the National Health, privately at vast expense – or for the price of this book and a little determination.

There are a billion ways of relaxing – or none at all. It depends on you. If you think you can't relax you're probably right. Right now. But when you're ready, it's easy to learn.

The Mind / Body Meltdown

Years ago, I went to antenatal classes at the local kindergarten. The midwife told us to breathe deeply and picture white sand and clear blue seas, but her voice sounded like a dental drill.

Although it was winter, the heating went off just before we arrived and the chairs were designed for five-year-olds, not large ladies. What's more, the classes were in the dining hall and the smell of cabbage reminded me depressingly of my schooldays. The warm beach and lapping waves didn't stand a chance against reality.

Use both your body and your mind to relax – your *whole* body and your *whole* mind. Having half a mind to take a break,

or putting your feet up while you worry,
doesn't work. Stress leaks in through any
bit of you that isn't fully involved in the
relaxation process.

when I'm cleaning windows...

Plugging All The Gaps

The world comes to you through your senses of sight, hearing, smell, taste, and touch. If you happen to have any others, by all means use them too. Relaxation exercises work by shutting out external stress and closing down internal sources of it as well. So, if you don't use *all* your senses to relax, you may find that while you're concentrating on one, anxiety is building up somewhere else. Beautiful movies in your mind won't do anything for you if you're still running a horror film soundtrack.

Technicolour Surround Sound with Popcorn

Another thing to remember – you may know this already, but if not, experiment with it – is that everyone has a preference about which sense they use most. A lot of people see life in pictures; when they worry, they *see* road accidents or spiders or family rows in their minds. Then there are the people who rely more on what they hear; they will whine and nag themselves. And the people who get the feel of a situation before they see it or hear it, will get hot under the collar, twitchy, tense or downcast.

You may not know which is your strongest sense. In fact most of us use them all to some extent – so when you're ready to chill out, make sure you've got relaxation coming at you through all the channels, not just one. As you get to know yourself better, you will fine-tune your routine to fit your own preferences. But right now, cover all your bases.

Comfort Zone

Take care of physical feedback first:

~ Sit comfortably – some people relax
  lying down, but I fall asleep when I do
  that and falling asleep is not the same
  as deep relaxation.

~ Make sure the temperature is right
  for you.

~ Protect yourself from interruptions.

Soundtrack

You can't relax with a chorus of voices in your head discussing what's for dinner or asking whether you locked the door. You will learn to simply turn them off, but for now, just drown them out. There's plenty of New Age meditation music around, if that appeals to you. Choose whatever sounds put you in the right state (not a right old state). It might be Jazz or Gregorian Chants or Gospel. I knew one man who meditated to rugby songs and another one who just couldn't chill out unless he had Busta Rhymes playing loud enough to vibrate the ceiling.

Smell and Taste

Avoid smells that evoke an active response – good or bad, it doesn't matter. Baking bread is as distracting as a load of manure. Scented candles or fragrant plants are a good way to block this particular entrance to your mind – but check out the candles carefully: cheap ones smell like toilet cleaner. Like music, this is a prop you won't need for ever – although it's a nice extra if you have time and space.

The Rainbow

2 – 10 Minutes

~ The Rainbow exercise is based on *chakras*. Chakra is the Sanskrit word for wheel or disk – a spinning vortex of energy – and there are seven of them, relating to different points on the body, each with its own colour of the rainbow. For some people they have spiritual or psychic significance, for others they are simply a focus.

~ Think of a simple affirmation, like 'I am feeling peaceful now'. This will become an anchor if you say it to yourself every time you need to run this relaxation, and it will be incredibly useful when you need to chill out quickly.

~ Start at the red end of the spectrum.
   From the base of your spine, down to
   the soles of your feet, you are
   grounded, connected to the earth. Stay
   with that warm, red glow for as long as
   you want.

~ When your attention moves up to your
   hips you will notice the colour
   changing to orange as you are aware of
   the ambitions and desires in your life.
   However strong your needs may be, you
   are comfortable and in control.

~ The orange turns to yellow, as you
   centre yourself on your Hara (Chapter
   2). Your body floods with sunlight and
   you are aware of your need for survival,

of all the things you want, the outcomes you long for and the feelings you have for other people. Your desires are strong and you are powerful, but nothing is urgent.

~ As your attention rises through your body, the yellow turns gradually to green like spring leaves. The feeling around your heart is naturally calm. Stay with this feeling for a while.

~ When the green starts turning blue, move your attention up to your throat and find that you are thinking in words rather than pictures. If there's something you need to say, then say it now and move on.

~ Around your forehead the rainbow is indigo, a colour associated with intuition and deep perception.

~ Let the indigo blend to violet as your awareness rises to the crown of your head. At this point dismiss thoughts as they come and focus for as long as you can on the light.

~ When you are ready, take some deep breaths and sit quietly for a few more seconds before you get up and stretch.

HOW TO...

* Always start with your affirmation.
  Before long, just saying your special
  phrase will cue you up for a relaxation
  session and it will all become very easy.

* You need to experiment to find the
  ideal length of time for you. Longer
  isn't necessarily better. For some people
  two minutes is perfect, for others it
  may be six and a half. You'll know
  when it's right.

* Let the colours and rising focus of your
  attention support you and keep your
  mind or body from wandering.

* Block out potential sound and smell distractions by providing your own soothing ones. Eventually you won't need these and then you'll be able to do this exercise in the supermarket queue, on the train or while you're washing up.

* Do the Rainbow exercise every day for a while before you decide whether to keep it.

...DO IT

* Run this routine whenever you need it and whenever you don't. Do it once a day if you find it easy to take your time, and twice if you fly through it.

* It's a good idea to start it *before* the panic sets in. Do it while you're in the dentist's waiting room, don't wait until you're in the chair.

Chapter Five

Soothing Touches

Giving a massage can be a short term investment or a long term, compound interest investment.
YOKO MORADA

BENEFITS

∗ Massage has a big payoff for the person who gives it.

∗ Touch is a powerful, subtle way to communicate, and the key to success in any area of life is communication.

∗ Massage eases tension for both giver and receiver.

* A massage is a message that invites a positive response.

* Pausing for thought before offering a massage is a great opportunity to ask yourself what outcome you want. The insight you get from this pause for thought may be as good for you as the massage is for the other person.

BONUS

* It's less offensive to massage your own wrists and hands at work than to chew your pen, or smoke or pick your fingernails.

* Giving a massage at home uses more
  calories than having an argument and
  might improve your sex life.

I was chatting to a teacher recently and I noticed a mark on his hand. 'Have you got a dog?' I asked.

'No, one of the infants bit me when I was on playground duty,' he said.

I was horrified. 'Does that happen a lot?'

'Not often, but some kids have no personal boundaries – and we have to be careful about restraining them. We're hardly allowed to touch them at all now in case we're accused of molesting them.'

Another problem struck me. 'What happens if a little one is crying?' I asked him.

'Twenty years ago I could hug them, but that's not allowed any more.'

Obviously children need protection

from being caned or sexually assaulted –
but, on the other hand, well-fed babies in
institutions can die from lack of cuddles.
It's a shame that children apparently have
to be deprived of the physical contact they
need, and most adults could do with more
hugs as well.

The British have always been suspicious
of the power of touch – to us, an
advertisement for a MASSAGE means just
one thing. The fact that we confuse
touching with sex or aggression means we
miss out on a vital channel of
communication in business and social
situations.

Years ago, when I trained as a social
worker, my tutor took me on a home
visit to a depressed, elderly man. The

pensioner, huddled in his chair, looked at us suspiciously. My tutor immediately went over to the fluffy white dog asleep on the rug and stroked it, all the while maintaining eye contact with the old man. As the dog stretched out to enjoy the attention, her owner relaxed and started talking about his problems.

When we left I asked her what was going on. 'He was just lonely,' she said, 'he needs a hug, but it's unprofessional to hug your clients so I stroked his dog instead. He got the message just the same.'

The Medium is the Massage

What's the difference between touching someone and massaging them? It's the difference between 'How are you?' and 'Come to dinner Tuesday'. The first simply acknowledges the other person, but the second demands an answer.

AMPPS – Attitude, Movement, Presence, Pressure, Situation

A successful massage depends on:

Attitude

~ When you're tired and frazzled, words can fail, but massage is a message that can't be ignored.

~ Before you offer a massage, ask yourself why. If there's no good, positive reason, don't do it. 'I want something that you don't want to give me' is not a good reason. If you get a positive answer like 'I think you need some TLC', or, 'You're too stressed to work with right now', keep that message in mind for the first few seconds of the massage.

~ Never massage someone you're angry with. Your hands will tell the truth.

Movement

~ Always keep one hand on the person you are massaging until you have finished – tell them when you are finishing.

~ Ask for feedback – at first you won't always know what feels good and what doesn't.

~ Give feedback – so your subject knows they have your attention as well as your hands.

~ Forget precision, this isn't a therapeutic massage. Do what feels right, keep it slow, gentle and non-invasive. We do this naturally for our pets – why is it so difficult to stroke other human beings?

~ Repeat each massage movement slowly three to six times.

Presence

~ Always be present in the moments of massage. Don't massage someone when your mind is somewhere else – or with someone else.

~ Reassure your subject that you are with them by making eye contact when you start and finish.

Pressure

~ Your subject should be lower than you
  so you can apply pressure gently and
  evenly.

~ Use your hands. You can buy little
  wooden things with rollers but they
  depersonalise the experience. You can
  only feel tension and reaction by using
  your hands.

Situation

~ Some organisations employ masseurs
to wander around their offices in the
hope of reducing RSI (Repetitive Strain
Injury) and some Japanese bars in
London offer mini massages with the
beer and sushi. It's definitely becoming
as acceptable as eating and drinking in
public – but there are rules:

  o stick to feet, neck and, maybe, hands

  o don't use oil.

~ Remembering the rules of relaxation in
Chapter 4, cover as many sensory
channels (besides touch) as you can:

o ask your subject to close her eyes

o use your voice to soothe, maintain contact and provide feedback

o perfumed oils and music take care of hearing and smell during home massages, but don't use them at work – you'll distract everybody else.

The Classic Massage

2 – 5 Minutes

You see this in films – one person sits and the other leans over them, massaging their neck – usually while trying to talk them into something (rubbing in the message). If your massage has a message, make sure it's positive. (Attitude)

~ With both hands on the left shoulder of your subject, use circular thumb movements along the back of the shoulder towards the neck. Continue round the back of the neck and along to the edge of the right shoulder. Work your way back.

~ Move both hands to the nape of the neck and work up and down the top of the spine, using circular thumb movements on either side.

~ With both hands at the nape again, press up and down the neck.

Foot Massage

5 Minutes

~ Sit down facing your subject and place one of their feet on your knee.

~ Run both hands over the foot until you get a feel for it. Ask how it feels to your subject.

~ Press around the ankle and the back of the heel.

~ Move back to the top of the foot and work down between the bones, firmly but gently.

~ With circular thumb movements, massage the sole of the foot – soles can be ticklish so press firmly.

~ Avoid toes – unless you know your subject well.

~ When you finish one foot, transfer your hands one at a time to the other foot.

HOW TO…

* This is just to get you started and I
  deliberately haven't given precise
  movements – these are just suggestions.
  Practise on someone who isn't
  expecting too much while you develop
  your *own* movements and timing.

* Practise on your own hands and feet to
  get an idea for what feels good.

...DO IT

* When you have your own style, by
  heart and in your hands, do it as often
  as you can and see what happens. The
  quality of your relationships will
  certainly change for the better –
  provided that your intentions are clear
  and good. But the changes may not
  always be ones you expect, so expect to
  be surprised.

Chapter Six

Time Management

Time is on your side, yes it is.
THE ROLLING STONES

BENEFITS

Time Management takes off the pressure. You may still not get *everything* done – but you will get the *important* things done.

BONUS

Time Management makes great use of downtime.

* Get yourself organised while you commute.

* Dump your problems on paper at bedtime and you're more likely to get a good night's sleep.

* Run through your Time Management plan first thing in the morning and make use of the time you spend trying to get out of bed.

When I worked for a large international telecommunications company I noticed that the Human Resources (HR) Department was frequently overwhelmed by daily crises. These crises distracted staff from important stuff like designing retirement packages for middle management and monitoring incentive schemes for sales executives. During my first week I remember being astonished when the department was thrown into chaos because the Finance Director's wife's parrot died in transit to Hong Kong. This formidable lady was determined that the HR executive who booked the flight should be fired and the airline sued, so

everyone scurried frantically around
passing bits of this trivial problem on like
hot cakes.

The following day, a meeting was
called – it was obvious that this was the
tip of a big problem iceberg. The HR
Director sent us on a Time Management
course and we all came back with diaries
bigger than our briefcases. These diaries
had project charts, activity wheels with
sections for work, personal development,
exercise, relationship development,
recreation and even sleep. There were
boxes to tick and five columns for every
job to be done. There was a priority
column, a category column (type of job),
an estimated time column (how long you

thought it would take), a real time column (how long it did take), and a satisfaction or results column (how you felt about that completed task on a scale of one to ten). There was even a special pack of coloured pens to fill in the diagrams.

A few months later the Department was bumbling along in the same inefficient and well meaning way it always had, while the mega diaries gathered dust. One lunchtime when everybody else was out, the consultant who ran the TM courses phoned to see if she could sell us some more training. 'I think we've all done Time Management', I said, looking at my diary which I was using as a mouse mat.

'Oh, I'm not doing Time Management any more,' she said airily, 'I'm doing Stress Management now – there's a lot of stress in workplaces at the moment.'

'It's probably caused by having to find time to fill in that diary every day.' I said.

The List

I know what you're thinking: 'Is that it? Just a list? I do that anyway!' Everybody makes lists and most Time Management programmes just teach you to make more complicated ones. But the more complicated they are, the less likely you are to use them. There's an old saying:

> *List it, lose it, clear your brain*
> *Then, tomorrow, start again.*

Lists can be a brain flushing exercise. They make us feel better, but don't get things done.

~ Use a LIST instead of just making one.

~ Time your LIST not your tasks.

   Look
   Itemise
   Sort
   Tick

Look

2 Minutes

~ Look at what you *want* to do with your life over the next 24 hours and write it down.

~ Look at what you *need* to do.

~ Look at what you *ought* to do.

~ Look at what you *must* do.

Check through all four categories – even though you won't necessarily write in all four. For example:

LOOK	ITEMISE	SORT	TICK

Want to do
Buy shoes
Go to the cinema
Do some gardening
Phone a friend

Need to do
Take some exercise
Have a rest
Go for a haircut

Ought to do
Visit an elderly relative
Service the car
Finish decorating the hall

Must do
Complete work assignment
Buy dog food
Call plumber or fix leak
Take the kids swimming

Itemise

2 Minutes

Look at what you've written and apply the four 4 Ds:

~ Do it.

~ Ditch it.

~ Defer it.

~ Delegate it.

Most of us feel a sense of satisfaction when a task is completed – but you can get a very similar endorphin rush from ditching, deferring (provided you write it down) and delegating. For example:

LOOK	ITEMISE	SORT	TICK
Want to do			
Buy shoes	*Defer*		
Go to the cinema	*Do*		
Do some gardening	*Defer*		
Phone a friend	*Do*		
Need to do			
Take some exercise	*Ditch*		
Have a rest	*Ditch*		
Go for a haircut	*Defer*		
Ought to do			
Visit an elderly relative	*Do*		
Service the car	*Do*		
Finish decorating the hall	*Delegate*		
Must do			
Complete work assignment	*Do*		
Buy dog food	*Delegate*		
Call plumber or fix leak	*Do*		
Take the kids swimming	*Delegate*		

Sort

2 Minutes

This is sometimes called the Sweet Jar exercise because it is like an empty jar and a pile of sweets – king size Mars Bars, gobstoppers, liquorice allsorts, toffees, Smarties, Tic Tacs, hundreds and thousands, and sherbet.

If you filled it up with Mars Bars first, you could still fit a few gobstoppers in around them. Then there might be room for a few liquorice allsorts and toffees, and when you couldn't get any more of those in, the Smarties would probably slip down the sides. When no more Smarties would go in, the Tic Tacs would probably trickle into cracks and then there might still be

space to slip the hundreds and thousands in. Even when the jar seemed completely full, the sherbet would filter through, like water, filling up the last tiny cracks.

What's the point? That you can always fit more into a day than you think? No, it's how you do it that matters. Always put the big things in first. It's so tempting, first thing in the morning, to get the little bits and pieces out of the way. Not because they're most important, but because they're easier to face than the big stuff. And before you know it, the day's gone and a couple of the top priority items still loom over you. Here's the second stage of the list:

LOOK	ITEMISE	SORT	TICK
Want to do			
Buy shoes	*Defer*	0	
Go to the cinema	*Do*	4	
Do some gardening	*Defer*	0	
Phone a friend	*Do*	3	
Need to do			
Take some exercise	*Ditch*	0	
Have a rest	*Ditch*	0	
Go for a haircut	*Defer*	0	
Ought to do			
Visit an elderly relative	*Do*	3	
Service the car	*Do*	3	
Finish decorating the hall	*Delegate*	3	
Must do			
Complete work assignment	*Do*	1	
Buy dog food	*Delegate*	2	
Call plumber or fix leak	*Do*	1	
Take the kids swimming	*Delegate*	1	

Tick

30 Seconds

The tick gives the best endorphin release of all the Time Management activities so it's a great motivator. Get yourself addicted to that little high – it builds the motivation you need to keep this good habit going.

HOW TO...

* Use one diary (or electronic organiser) for everything. If it's a diary, choose a plain one with at least one day to a page so you can draw up your own layout. Make it light enough to carry around.

...DO IT

* Do it every day, even on holiday. Dump it in the diary, don't burden your brain.

Chapter Seven

No-Sweat Workouts

Being active makes you more attractive.
Pete Cohen

BENEFITS

* Regular, steady exercise is good for your body and your mind.

* It reduces the risk of heart disease and lots of other major and minor illnesses too.

* It makes you feel cheerful by releasing endorphins. Some doctors prescribe it for depression.

BONUS

As well as making you look and feel better, walking and cycling (great forms of exercise) have practical spin-offs.

* They save bus and train fares, parking fines and car maintenance

* They are the fastest way to get around in cities.

* They are great stress relievers.

A colleague of mine came to work one morning yawning. She slumped in her chair with a cup of coffee and said 'I just can't wake up'.

'Late night?' I asked.

'No, not really. I never can get going first thing.'

'Why don't you try walking to work?' I suggested. 'You must be less than a mile from the office – and you could walk along the river. It might wake you up.'

She looked confused. 'Why would I want to do that? I don't need to lose weight and the car parking comes with the job. Besides which, if I'm tired already, walking to work is only going to make it worse.'

A lot of people think exercise is only necessary for losing weight and train strikes. But, sports scientist and slimming guru Pete Cohen says: 'Your body was designed for one thing and one thing only – to move'.

In fact, Pete has taught me a lot – one of the most important things being that useful exercise is regular, steady and comfortable. He uses the Fat Jar to help people get more activity into their lives.

The Fat Jar

10 Minutes

OK, I cheated, Pete originally said 15 minutes. But you can fill the Ten-Minute Fat Jar as many times a day as you like, as long as you use time you'd normally spend being inactive.

~ Get a jar.

~ Put 20p in it every time you take ten minutes of continuous, aerobic exercise.

~ Walking to work or the shops or the pub is fine – at a good, steady pace. Breathe in through your nose. Panting means you're overdoing it. Breathing through your nose shows you're exercising at the right level and it's also a way of increasing your breathing capacity. Which is good for your health as well as your state of mind. Remember Chapter 1?

~ The advantage of a Fat Jar is that you can see how much exercise you're taking – you will notice when you aren't getting as much and it's a visual, motivational reminder to put more movement into your life.

~ When the Fat Jar is full, spend the money on a treat.

Stretch

One Minute

Animals are supposed to know what's good for them and all animals stretch regularly. In fact, some cats don't do much else! Human beings, on the other hand, don't stretch much at all. It's considered rude at board meetings or dinner parties – though it might loosen up business and social situations quite a bit. Have you noticed that a stretch is often followed by a smile? It makes you feel good.

You can just go right ahead and stretch any way your instinct takes you, or you can do the official version:

~ Stand feet together, stretch as tall as
  you can.

~ Interlock your fingers behind your
  head, elbows sticking out at your sides.
  Breathe in.

~ Breathe out, turn palms upwards,
  stretch your arms and clench your outer
  leg muscles.

~ Relax and breathe in.

~ On your next out breath, bring your
  hands down to your hips, maintaining
  the lift on your spine.

~ Take your hands off your hips and stretch forward, with your back curving over and your head in line with your spine. Place your hands beside your feet and look down.

~ Gradually unroll yourself back to your upright, stretched tall position. Relax.

The Quick Fix Warm Up

4 Minutes

Do each of these 3 to 5 times.

~ Face a wall with the heel of one foot on the floor and the ball of the foot against the wall. Lean forward into the wall and feel the calf muscles stretch. Do the same with the other leg.

~ Stand on your left leg holding your right ankle up with your right hand. Put your left hand on a wall for balance and pull up on your right leg until you feel your muscles stretch. Repeat the other side.

~ Place your right heel on a chair or anything slightly above waist height. Lean towards that leg, keeping your back straight and feel your hamstring stretch. Repeat the other side.

~ Roll both shoulders forward and back in a circular motion.

~ Stand sideways to a wall with your right arm stretched out to touch the wall at shoulder height. Turn away from the wall until you feel the stretch in your arm and shoulder. Repeat.

~ Finish with a full body stretch.

The Quick Fix Workout

6 Minutes

Do this as often as you like but make it at least once a day if you want to feel the benefit.

~ Lie on your back with your feet flat on the floor and knees bent. Cross your arms over your chest and use your abdominal muscles to pull your chest to your knees.

~ Lie on your stomach and use your lower back muscles to lift your shoulders off the ground and back as far as you can towards your feet. Keep your feet on the ground and your arms at your sides. If you really need to, use your arms (as in a pushup) to raise your shoulders from the ground.

~ Lying on your stomach lift your left arm and right leg, hold for one or two seconds and lower. Repeat on the other side.

~ Stand up with your feet shoulder width apart. With your back straight, bend your knees to almost 80 degrees, then stand upright again. Keep your rib cage lifted and your abdominal muscles tucked in.

~ Standing with your back straight put your left foot in front of you. Bend both knees and lower your body until your right knee almost touches the floor. Stand up again and repeat the other side.

~ Lie flat on your back on your bed with your feet just extended over the edge. Press your heels, back of legs and bum down on the bed by squeezing your hamstring muscles.

~ Stand up, and use one hand to balance yourself on the wall and raise both heels from the floor holding yourself upright on the balls of your feet.

~ Lie on your stomach with your body straight. Raise your body on your hands and the balls of your feet until your arms are almost straight. Use your knees if you are unfit.

HOW TO...

* Anchor an all-over stretch routine to a regular activity – whenever you wash your hands for example.

* Learn all the routines and see which ones easily become automatic for you.

...DO IT

* Regularity matters. Exercise makes you feel better and look better if you do it regularly. But, if you have to go to a special place and wear special clothes and make a special effort, it may not become part of your life. Exercise should be as instinctive as eating and sleeping.

Note: Remember to consult your doctor before starting a new stretch or exercise routine, especially if you haven't been taking much exercise recently.

Chapter Eight

Home Help with Feng Shui

Have nothing in your houses that you do not know to be useful, or believe to be beautiful.
WILLIAM MORRIS

BENEFITS

* Feng Shui is an excuse to stand back and look at your living space from a completely different point of view – one that's free from the influence of fashion, budgets or other people.

* Your environment affects you and reflects you. You may not know

whether the house looks dingy because you feel depressed or you feel depressed because the house is dingy – but try a new coat of paint on the walls before you rush into therapy.

BONUS

* Rearranging the furniture has always been a guaranteed mood enhancer – Feng Shui can be a cheap and easy way to do it.

G etting to grips with your physical
 fitness, sorting out your
relationships, managing your time and
learning to relax is fine. But don't ignore
your external influences. You can't do
much about your neighbourhood, your
route to work or the transport you use, but
a little effort can make a lot of difference
to the places where you spend most time
– your home and workplace.

Most of us live with things that don't
suit our lifestyle or just aren't useful any
more; things people have given us and we
don't like but don't like to throw out.
Even expensive designer homes are just
junk when they're out of fashion.

I had a brown shag pile carpet in the 1970s which was depressing to look at and impossible to keep clean with three small children and a cat around. I hated it for years, but only threw it out when I discovered my daughter's friends had invented a game where they scored points for the number of edible objects they could find in it.

The Dinner Party Test

Feng Shui's fashionable, but don't let that put you off. It's fine as long as it's applied by people who are fully qualified in commonsense and scepticism. If not, it can easily get out of control. I recently went to dinner with friends and when I visited the downstairs loo, I switched on the light to find a papyrus plant in the toilet and a wind chime in place of the chain.

I rejoined them at the table and pointed out that they were lucky I wasn't drunk or it might have been a disaster. Jane looked uncomfortable and said 'actually, we had the house Feng Shui'd last week and the consultant told us that what with the direction of the toilet and the water and everything we were literally flushing our finances down the drain'.

'So are you getting richer now?' I asked.

Her husband exploded – 'we need to be – I got the * * * * consultant's bill this morning'.

If you end up with something that embarrasses or bankrupts you, you've almost certainly got it wrong. Apply the Dinner Party Test and try a few minor adjustments on your friends and family before you install a fountain on the landing or move all the doors.

It doesn't matter whether you

understand or believe in Feng Shui or not.
The important thing is to start thinking
about whether your living space actually
works for you or whether it dictates your
lifestyle. See if some small changes make
you feel more comfortable, dynamic,
restful, creative – or whatever you want to
be.

Once you start asking yourself whether
you have enough personal space, the right
amount of light, too many dark corridors
or poky unlit corners, change begins to
happen. Have you noticed how a cat
instinctively knows the best places in the
house – the warmest corners with the best
vantage points? Human beings aren't as
instinctive as that, we need to *think* about
our environment.

*Let's get to grips with what's going down
on the outside!*
THE ANTI-COUNSELLING LEAGUE

Feng Shui in its gentler manifestations
is a kind of mystical common sense.
According to Eastern wisdom there is
more to the world than we can see, feel,
hear, smell and taste, there's also the
silent breath of *chi*.

Chi is the underlying flow of electromagnetic energy. The force that links humans to their surroundings. The ideal is to have a smooth flow of chi, avoiding frenetic energy swirls or stagnant pools. Living spaces should also have a balance of calm *Yin* energy and extrovert *Yang* energy. Have you noticed that some homes feel stressful while others are dull and depressing?

Buying Your Own House

5 Minutes

Pretend you are buying your own house all over again and the estate agent is showing you around for the first time. Walk from room to room and look for:

~ negative (or positive) atmospheres and feelings in particular areas

~ dark or gloomy places

~ clutter

~ oddly shaped rooms with corners cut off

~ corridors that act like wind tunnels
   (Victorian terraces with halls that
   go right through the house are often
   like this)

~ over-bright, uncoordinated, stressful
   rooms

~ any places you hardly go into or use
   (why?).

Now that you've made your assessment,
see what you can do to improve the
situation.

Getting the Chi to Flow

10 Minutes

~ Plants can speed up or slow down
  energy. Being alive, they have their
  own radiant energy and they freshen
  the atmosphere. Use differently shaped
  plants for different effects, spiky ones
  with pointed leaves liven up neglected
  corners where chi stagnates. Plants
  with rounded floppy leaves smooth the
  chi around jutting corners. They can
  regulate the flow of chi in passageways.

~ Chi reacts like light, so you can work
  miracles with mirrors.

  ○ reflect the chi and change its
    direction with shiny surfaces.

- o regulate light and complete irregularly partitioned rooms.

- o make sure that mirrors don't cut off people's heads or split reflections.

~ Light is very important and light
shining upwards is supposed to
encourage an uplifting atmosphere.
Bright lights are believed to stimulate
chi while dimmer lights slow it down.
Whatever you think about this, look at
your lights and try different effects to
see if they alter your mood.

~ Most people agree that colours affect
them: blue is cold (or restful,
depending on your point of view), red
is hot and makes you hungry, a room
painted black could be quite depressing
– and so on. In spite of that, we still
put the strangest colours in our homes
sometimes – just because they are
fashionable. Remember the purple,

orange and green wallpaper of the 1970s? And the dark red baths (at least the dirt didn't show). Even if you weren't there, you've probably seen examples of it somewhere. Feng Shui of course has its own colour coding:

- green for life, growth and vitality
- red for excitement and warmth
- yellow and brown for feelings of security.

But you don't have to accept these. Work out what effect colours have on you and use them to create calm bedrooms, lively living rooms and creative kitchens – or whatever suits your lifestyle.

Clear Clutter

10 Minutes

This is a Feng Shui classic. Have you ever said 'I'm just going outside to clear my head'? It's not just a question of fresh air – outdoors we are free of the clutter of domestic life. Have you ever noticed how a physical mess clogs your thoughts and slows you down? The Feng Shui theory is that clutter slows the chi energy and makes us less efficient – if nothing else, you can waste a lot of time just looking for things you've lost in an untidy environment.

HOW TO...

* You don't have to sort out your whole house in one day. Pace your space clearing exercise, ten minutes at a time, over a long period and you'll get into the habit of constantly reviewing your environment. That way you're less likely to be overtaken by cluttered corners, fading colours, dying plants and dusty surfaces.

...DO IT

* Start immediately with the Buying Your Own House exercise.

Chapter Nine

Dear Diary

A diary is a rope you weave to climb back up to the light. But you can be hanged with it too.
METIN KAHLEEL

BENEFITS

* A diary is a quick, cheap, easy way to find out what's going on in your life. You can't change things if you don't know about them.

* Writing a diary gives you an excuse for valuable quiet time.

BONUS

* The diary habit will hook you just for as long as you need it. It often self destructs if it becomes obsolete.

I f you could divide up what's going on in your head, what categories would there be?

(a) Time thinking constructively about your life, your hopes and dreams and when you're going to achieve them?

(b) Time full of anxiety about things left undone? People who let you down? Things and people you want and can't have, but you feel they would complete you and make you into something?

(c) Anaesthetised time – drugs, sleeping, watching too much TV, frantic activity, acquiring things you don't need?

If (a) doesn't amount to much compared with (b) and (c) maybe it's because life isn't living up to your expectations. But there's only one thing you can change and that's you. Whining about your partner, your children, your job or the trains running late may be justified, but won't improve the situation. In fact, it will probably make things worse.

The answer to most problems is better communication and a diary is an efficient way to communicate with yourself. A way to recognise the bits of yourself you like and the bits of yourself that are bent on self-sabotage, so that you can do some emotional spring cleaning. A way of recognising the insights and opportunities that are offered to us all each day, but which we often miss because we're too busy watching EastEnders or trying to change somebody else's behaviour instead of our own.

Go and buy yourself a diary now – don't use the same one you're using for time management because this self-space diary shouldn't have dates. There will be days when you want to write more than 24 hours' worth and there will be days you miss altogether. Choose a notebook that pleases you and a pen you like the feel of. Keep them apart from the jumble of the rest of your life and treat yourself to the time to write.

Maybe you could use up some downtime – is there anything you regularly do that you wish you didn't?

Substitute the diary for some of that time and see what happens.

An old friend of mine was delighted when her diary was published – she'd led an interesting life. But when I saw her two years later and I asked her how it was selling she told me it was selling well and she wished she had never written it.

'How can you say that?' I asked her. 'Everybody wants to be published, don't they?'

'Looking back', she said, 'I can see that every word I wrote was written not for me, but for my imaginary future audience. If I'd written it for me it wouldn't have been published, but I'd have gained something much more valuable and learned a lot of things I might never learn now. My

publishers want volume two', she said,
'but I told them to whistle for it, volume
two is for my eyes only'.

The other day she sent me a copy of her
latest novel with a note that said, 'I finally
learned the difference between writing for
me and writing for other people'.

Don't feel your diary is second rate
because nobody else will read it. You are
worth the effort and you can write it any
way that makes sense to you.

The Self-Improver

5 Minutes

This is a very focused way of writing a diary.

~ List the values which are most important to you.

~ Write down your goal in life – if there is more than one, keep the list short.

~ Is your goal consistent with your values? If for example, your values and goals looked like this:

Values
  o involvement with your children's development and education

o   personal fitness a top priority
    (amateur triathlete).

Goals

o   to be rich beyond the dreams of
    avarice in five years' time
o   to establish a career path with
    development opportunities.

The first goal is unlikely to be realistic if
you're starting from scratch and are
committed to young children and a high
level of personal fitness. Getting rich quick
takes time and dedication – you might
have to compromise your values.

The second goal is more likely – if you
haven't made your millions yet, perhaps
it's because you haven't found your

vocation. If you're prepared to work towards it gradually you may have more chance of getting what you want.

~ When you come up with a goal that is consistent with your personal values, write down what's stopping you from achieving that goal right now. Next make a list of twenty things you could do to bring you closer to that goal in the next six months.

Up Close and Personal

2 – 10 Minutes

Before you start writing this version of the diary, make headings on the page to prompt you.

HEADING	EXAMPLE
Goals	*No solitaire on the computer until the project is finished.*
Achievements	*Managed a whole day without smoking.*
Gifts	*Sun came out for the match. Great joke on the internet.*
Insights	*Suddenly realised that I nag my daughter exactly the same way my mother nagged me!*
Challenges	*Completing the project tomorrow. Getting the car serviced. Getting to the Board Meeting.*
Action	*Rearrange filing system and clear out paperwork.*

HOW TO...

* Whichever diary you choose, do it when you are alone, not on a train or in a room with people walking through.

...DO IT

* It doesn't have to be every day, just every two or three days. It should start to weave a coherent thread through your life if it's going to have any strength to support you when you need it.

Chapter Ten

Sweet Dreams

*A good night's sleep is like money in the bank
– it gains interest.*

MARIANNE MAKEPEACE

BENEFITS

Giving yourself some encouragement and
talking yourself through your concerns
before you sleep, then debriefing yourself
thoroughly when you wake up is an
effective way to:

* solve problems

* collate and sort relevant life
  information

* pick up data your conscious mind may have missed during the day.

BONUS

* These exercises use the ultimate in downtime – working for you while you sleep.

Sleep is a problem-solving activity not an anaesthetic.

Most of my chapters start with a story but this last one doesn't because it's waiting for yours. Before you fall asleep tonight, ask yourself for some ideas about what you might do with the stuff in this chapter and see what happens, tonight, tomorrow night – or a fortnight from now. It will take as long as it takes, but when you start asking questions, you will get answers, when you're ready for them. Asleep or awake, keep an eye open for nice surprises because those are the ones that are easy to miss. Bad ones are harder to ignore.

The conscious mind is wonderful, and I'm all in favour of using it – taking our own decisions for example rather than accepting what other people or advertising agencies tell us to think. But the conscious mind was never meant to work alone. The most creative and resourceful people know their intellectual ability is a partnership of conscious and unconscious. They know that there is a part of their thinking that they can use but not control. It's true of scientists as well as artists – some great insights into the laws of the natural world have been made by dreamers whose mental laboratories were as important as their physical ones.

There are lots of problems in our every-day life that we can't possibly solve by conscious thought, because our minds can't handle enough data. Seven plus or minus two bits of information is apparently all we can cope with at a time.

But the subconscious can take a lot more than that and analyse it as well. Which is why our dreams often seem so confusing – there are just too many things going on in them at once. We have to ask our subconscious to pitch in and come up with some answers.

Maybe we could stop thinking altogether and let our subconscious minds get on with organising our lives. Some people do that, but it's called insanity and it's not a comfortable way to live. The subconscious mind doesn't function well alone, it needs the conscious mind to act as a protocol gauge to interface with the real world.

A Mental Work Out

Sleeping is neither a waste of time nor a temporary escape from life's problems. Margaret Thatcher apparently slept very little while she was Prime Minister. Perhaps if she had allowed her subconscious to participate more often in her decisions she would have been a different kind of politician. Or maybe she wouldn't have been a politician at all.

If you think sleep is a great opportunity to do some problem-solving and self-affirmation, then it's worth preparing yourself to get the most benefit from it. Just as you might warm up before exercising. But preparation for mental exercise is the reverse of what you do

when you work out: the five-minute cool
down happens before you start to sleep
and the five-minute warm up when you
wake.

Basic Cool Down

2 – 5 Minutes

How long does it take you to fall asleep?
Are you gone as soon as your head hits
the pillow? Or do you toss and turn,
anxious about how tired you will feel in
the morning if you don't nod off soon?

If you're a fast sleeper, run through
these exercises while you're cleaning your
teeth instead of waiting to get into bed.
But if you're an anxious insomniac, treat
them as a soothing ritual, lulling you to
sleep, trusting in the power of your own
mind to sustain you.

These are the questions to ask; don't try
to stay awake for the answers – although
some will come immediately into your
mind.

~ What have I learned from today?

~ What have I done today that was positive – for someone else, or for myself?

~ How might today be an investment for my future? Was there a significant meeting, an insight, an opportunity?

~ What could I do to make the most of something that happened today?

~ Do I owe myself, or anyone else, an apology for anything today?

~ What six things made me happy today? These don't have to be big deals like winning the lottery. A smile, a flash of sunshine, a perfect cup of tea, a shop window, a flower, a goldfish...

Problem Solver

2 Minutes

Asking for a solution to a problem before sleeping is more likely to work if you structure your request and set up a framework for the answer. You won't need this every night (hopefully) – although it works for small niggles as well as big dilemmas.

~ If something is bugging you, don't put it on the shelf while you sleep and pick it up in the morning. Put it into words, if you can, and ask your sleeping, subconscious mind to work on it.

~ If you don't know exactly what's bothering you, ask for a definition first and leave the solution for later.

~ If you don't feel like sleeping yet and want to engage with the problem consciously before you sleep here are some useful questions:

   o What does this problem do for me?

   o Why haven't I solved it yet?

   o What first step could I take towards solving it?

   o How will I know when I'm ready to take that step?

   o What am I willing to change to solve this problem?

   o What am I not willing to change to solve it?

Wake Up Call

2 – 5 Minutes

People often do this while they lie in bed in the morning waiting for the alarm to go off. But if you sleep right up to the alarm and time is tight, it's another one to do while you clean your teeth.

~ If I went to sleep last night with a question in mind, am I any closer to an answer now? (If you don't have that answer yet, don't chase it. Wait until it comes.)

~ What am I happy about in my life? It doesn't have to be large or wonderful. Small happinesses count.

~ What am I excited about?

~ What am I proud of?

~ What am I grateful for?

~ What am I committed to – what matters most to me?

~ Who do I love?

~ Who loves me?

The Wonderful Me Routine

1 Minute

Top and tail your day with affirmations.
Never let the sun go down on a quarrel or
a misunderstanding with yourself. Give
yourself a bit of encouragement before
you sleep and welcome yourself back to
life when you wake. When I first learned
about self-affirmation, years ago, I used
affirmations out of books because I was
much too self-conscious to invent my
own. Then I visited a friend in Los Angeles
and noticed that every mirror in her house
had a post-it note on it: 'Yes! I am
beautiful,' on her dressing table, 'I am a
warm and wonderful woman,' in the
bathroom and 'I am poised and
confident', on the mirror in the hall.

'Aren't you embarrassed?' I asked her. She looked at me as if I was mad.

After that I was a bit less wary of them although I still don't stick them anywhere but in my own mind. I can imagine what my children and their friends would make of an opportunity like that. It's just not British – and it's pretty uncool too.

There are two rules for affirmations.

~ They must be positive.

~ They must be in the present tense.

'I am not going to be such a wimp tomorrow', will not do. 'I am strong and loving, powerful and loved',[1] is fine. Put together your own words that match your needs and strengths.

HOW TO...

* Design yourself a comfortable lead-in phrase to use at night: 'sleep is an adventure from which I shall wake up wiser and more resourceful', or 'I am free to dream and take part in my dreams and bring parts of my dreams back to my waking life'.

* You can use some of these night-time routines together with the diary in Chapter 9. Writing down insights and affirmations sometimes makes the whole process seem more real and valuable.

---

[1] Susan Jeffers, *Feel the Fear and Do It Anyway* (Arrow, 1991)

...DO IT

* Design yourself a bedtime/waking up
  routine, even if it's only a couple of
  sentences, and use it for a month
  before you decide whether or not it's
  for you. It's more valuable and
  inspirational when it's part of your life.

Now what?

If there are some ideas you really liked or some techniques that intrigued you, and you would like to spend more than ten minutes a day with them, give us a call at *Human Capital 020 8241 2266*. We can give you some ideas and contact details by phone or send you information.

The Human Capital Helpline for general enquiries is open nine to five from Monday to Friday and you can leave messages at any time. You can also fax us your name and address on 020 8241 2268 or email us on *info@humcap.co.uk*

List of Exercises